The Ballad of Lorianna, Ever Brush Away The Sleep, To Winter and other poems

Christopher Laverty

Contents

TO BEAUTY 5

THE MOONLIGHT HOURS 6

MUSIC OVER STILL WATER 7

A NOCTURNAL WANDERING 8

THE SHAMISEN 9

FALLEN DAYS 10

ABYSS OF DOUBT 11

LAST NIGHT 12

TO A BLACKBIRD 13

THE BALLAD OF LORIANNA 14

TO SOLITUDE 15

LORDS OF THE TEMPEST 17

TO WINTER 18

THE MUSIC OF THE NIGHT 20

THE VALLEY OF MELANCHOLIA 21

A NIGHT ON THE MOORS 24

SNOWBOUND 26

BY A WATERFALL 27

TWO CITIES 28

DO NOT WAKE HIM 29

THE IDLE HOURS 30

TWO FLOWERS 31

OVER OCEANS ROARING 32

ON THE UK LEAVING THE EU 33

THE PILLAR OF TEARS 34

ON ANIMALS 35

DRINK NOT TOO DEEP 36

SPIRITED UPON YOUR WINGS 37

EVER BRUSH AWAY THE SLEEP 39

THE CHILDREN OF THE SERPENT 41

IN DESPONDENCY 43

EMELIE 44

A BUTTERFLY I THOUGHT I SAW 45

ON VISITING NORTH DEVON IN
OCTOBER 47

MODERN BARDS 48

BIRD OF DESTINY 50

BLEMISHES 52

APPLE BLOSSOM GIRL 53

ON SEEING AN OPEN CASKET 54

ON SEEING MANCHESTER AT DAWN 55

THE GARDEN TOAD 56

DOWN ON THE HEATH 57

TO LIBERTY 58

THOUGHTS ON HOME WHILE ABROAD 59

OLD TALES I HAVE TURNED 60

COULD I CAST SPELLS 61

ON SEEING THE AOSTA VALLEY 62

TWO SPRINGS 63

ON WAKING IN A VALLEY IN AVEYRON 64

THE VILLAGE PLAGUE 65

TO FRIENDSHIP 66

THE HORSEMEN OF THE NORTH 67

TO BEAUTY

The lights of truth that faithful hung on high -
that lit the restless nights with sacred glow,
sleepless beacons, to mariners below
adrift in storm - in clouds now shrouded lie;
lost seas they sail beneath a starless sky.
The Muses of sylvan song - long ago
fled their valley; listless winds there blow,
once fertile springs of Helicon run dry.
But if, when lost in pathless woods alone,
perpetual twilight should my spirit seize -
if, in the land where fleeting shadows groan,
beauty forgotten lies, that might bring ease,
then it is my good fortune, to have known
your sainted balm, while carving rhymes like these.

THE MOONLIGHT HOURS

We'll no more pass the moonlight hours
by the riverside,
or share a silence as we stroll
beneath the colonnade.

Or shelter take from sudden showers,
or watch the settling tide,
or lie still when we moments stole
in some forgotten shade.

Those tender days, of light and shade -
the fading summer stole;
and so we'll no more pass the moonlight hours
by the riverside.

MUSIC OVER STILL WATER

Sleepless he walked beneath the wakeful sky;
a bright true crowd he saw - and envied them,
that in long life burn, and lone ease lie,
or fellowship gather; each silent gem

cheering the blindness that envelops us -
here for a blinking eye, a stolen dream.
Then suddenly there came - breaking the hush -
sweet music drifting on a nearby stream,

accosting him through balmy air. It stirred
his downcast spirit; a windless world he felt
and passing yet eternal moments heard,
and for a moment, with the stars he dwelt.

A NOCTURNAL WANDERING

Beneath the revelling moon - that trips the lake,
and does our waking world of shadows paint -
with tuneful pipe he spun the pale light faint,
he spun a song for her, only to wake

to sunlight cold and grey, in which his tune
lifeless lay; which though he threw, then wishing
it to forget - it followed him - while wandering,
late and lone, beneath the revelling moon.

THE SHAMISEN

One night I met a traveller,
here from an oriental land;
he little spoke, this wanderer,
and held a Shamisen in his hand.
His fingers danced across its strings,
the music told of far-off things:

of an exotic summer haze,
and rhythm of a rural pace;
timeless, gentle, carefree days,
and bustle of a marketplace,
where people talk and laugh and sigh,
hurry - or watch the world go by.

The music ceased, his hands fell still,
with silent nod he bid goodnight.
That morning, while I climbed a hill,
I hummed the tune with footsteps light.
Though fading memory might it steal,
its essence still I'll faintly feel.

FALLEN DAYS

They stole from heaven fire to meet their needs;
raised up, they less felt nature's fitful lash,
whose pitiless waves their hopes on rocks would dash;
knowledge then bloomed - near wisdom's withered seeds,

as soon they fought themselves with crimson creeds,
and always, somewhere, could be seen the flash,
and heard the distant din of armies clash,
while cenotaphs with glory shrined their deeds.

The ruins of their ancient realm we saw;
technology, from unremembered days,
lies lost; vines clasp their colonnades; a haze
of fallen palaces, temples, courts of law;

their libraries, whose lessons lay unlearnt,
in the midnight of their madness burnt.

ABYSS OF DOUBT

I knew one once, who wanted to believe
in something, and to bless it with the breath
with which he played his pipe, and made it weave
songs of youth and friendship, love and death.

And then he sang of wonders near and far,
of sights sublime, on mountains, hills, and sky,
sunsets, lightning, or a falling star -
and sighed, though he knew not the reason why.

He sought for something more, beyond this world
of shadows pale, but peered in an abyss
of doubt – and wished that he again was curled
in warming raiments of unknowing bliss.

LAST NIGHT

Last night I saw you - still young, turning your head
so gracefully, and laughing - robed in white -
as I on dream's soft fabric gently tread,
while stealing slices of sleep before daylight.
What was this hazy world - the uncharted land
of final rest, of neither space nor time?
Where we'll watch clouds, and every grain of sand,
until the waking bell of dawn should chime.
The trees no more would lose their leaves - no more
would birds depart for warmer climes, when we
together here will sit for evermore,
happy to escape life's troubled sea.
We'll hear dreamcatchers tinkle, and incense smell,
and hear the waves, and watch their gentle swell.

TO A BLACKBIRD

Blackbird - silent sat upon this headstone,
in this antique graveyard wide and drear;
so still - who so suddenly had flown;
do you come – when steals the twilight near -
the secrets of these sleeping souls to hear?

Poet of the shadows, wind swift bird,
tell what shady haunts you've made your home;
haunts your cheering bursts of song have heard?
What woods, fields – secluded - do you roam,
what forsaken dwellings overgrown?

Desolate hilltops, that enchantments hold,
lifeless villages - that know no Spring;
churches silent, whose statues have grown cold -
yet your voice to them some warmth might bring -
when to yourself, alone, you softly sing.

Blackbird – silent sat upon this headstone,
taking wing now to a nearby tree,
soon perhaps to midnight spots unknown;
gone now, gone far as the eye can see -
unheard tunes are sweeter in my memory.

THE BALLAD OF LORIANNA

Quaint Lorianna all adore;
around her dove white face
waves raven hair - with eyes where light
and darkness interlace.

Elusive nymph that all adore;
though she inhabits earth
she seems of lore; to hearts on fire
she unaware gives birth.

Sweet bitter nymph that all adore;
she's like the ocean's dim
retreating roar - and in her smile
lies tempests at a whim.

Shy sportive nymph that all adore;
a thousand hearts she'll tease
but then ignore - and all outpace
when she in forests flees.

Unearthly nymph that all adore;
my guileless heart gave chase -
torn to its core - I wished to win
the garland of her grace.

Quaint Lorianna all adore;
with love's divine disease
I sleepless pace, and thirst and bleed -
yet can't the pain appease.

TO SOLITUDE

Away with loneness - he whose winter bites,
who haunts the wasted wilderness and shores,
born in thunder on the misty moors;
who, bred by wolves, with howling fills the nights.
But bring his smooth browed sister Solitude,
decked with autumnal charms and plenitude;
with contemplation's brimming horn of flowers,
and baskets graced with fruit to fill the hours;
often you'll keep the company of dawn,
whose veils of innocence the woods adorn;
and sometimes there, with still and listening ear,
we might the secret songs of nature hear,
or by fountain sit, whose trickling sound
is where forgetful music may be found;
with closed eyes we'll feel it chase away
the phantoms of the mind that haunt the day;
and 'til the birds' soft choir the daylight greets,
we'll walk along the cool and silent streets,
that slumber in the dark with shutters down,
until the traffic will the quietness drown;
or we will walk the idle hours at night
beneath the naked sky; the only light
the lamps that blink beneath the smog and clouds;
and night is human – thoughts arise in crowds
in minds astir like beehives, while hearts swell
like glow worms' tails; there unseen creatures dwell
in graveyard, cricket green, and old inn,
whose chants arise to sooth the daily din;
we'll watch the botanical garden's calm cascades

dance on the moonlit paths and palisades;
hear murmurings of exotic plants and trees,
stirred in the tingling darkness by the breeze;
smell scents of herbs – of rosemary, sage and thyme,
that make the air tell of a distant clime.
But now I hear the mournful sounding train
rousing night, and sigh of passing plane,
as Solitude – to wintry chill you grow;
I feel its sharp breath through my window blow,
and round my door; the hand of loneness cold -
an anguish of the body - takes iron hold;
so now the spring of company I yearn,
but will to sister Solitude return.

LORDS OF THE TEMPEST

Lords of the tempest – ruling wind and rain
that lash eternally your mountain peak,
feel you the hearts of humans that you pain?
They are your marionettes when you chaos wreak
and dash on rocks their reason; when on bleak

dead waters of despondency they're bourne,
by raging waves ungovernable thrown -
when cast on island shores that know no dawn -
or in the mouth of your maelstrom blown,
as you summon whirlwinds from your throne.

Lords of the tempest – through your sleepless nights
the mariner sails; he hears your thunder peal
over the beckoning deep; can guiding lights
be traced within the stars the dark reveal,
as he steadfast steers the sea swept wheel?

TO WINTER

Autumn - your mild and melancholy strains
die in this air that's tinged with distant chill;
wreathed in your harvest yields that swelled the plains,
you fade from farms and fields whose barns lie still.
The pallid Sun and northern blasts commingle
to sweep away the remnants of your bloom,
while shivers the dreaming earth with inward tingle;
the earth - whose soil was once for seeds a womb,
now bride to Winter, you shall be their tomb.

Winter - descending from your glacial throne,
you cross the tremulous waters, laying siege
with hands of ice to all that Summer's grown,
binding the barren landscape to your liege.
Fierce creatures sleep out days grown aged and hoar,
buried beneath your gleaming vestal veils,
like soldiers holed in trenches waiting war,
while villages retreat to hearth and ales,
to games and laughter, fireside talk and tales.

You toil as nature's sculptor, keen and swift,
when in the deep mid-winter falls soft flakes;
then nimbly guiding their processional drift,
you carve your fine-spun work before dawn breaks,
decorating scenes with robes of white,
from which an intricate design you mould -
an alpine kingdom fashioned overnight,
beyond the scope of human craft - and bold
it glistens, like a promised land foretold.

In March how patient your encampment lies,
outside the fortified city of the Spring;
your primal beats still echo through the skies
over the bare branched woods where no birds sing.
While dead life strews the battlefield abysmal,
together you wage a struggle for the hand
of Earth, fair daughter of the Sun, though dismal
she lies beneath the frost, seedless as sand,
who this sunless empire must withstand.

Here comes the Sun unsheathed, and Winter flees.
To native mountain citadels you climb,
or, borne by chariot, past the Hebrides
you soar - back to the terrible Pole sublime.
Spring chases the vestiges of your cemetery,
while winds and showers nurse the earth to life,
whose peeping buds and blossoms will us free -
free us - who cannot free ourselves from strife,
while Winter in the human heart is rife.

THE MUSIC OF THE NIGHT

Tonight I've waited long for sleep, and lie frustrated – yet I I hear
a thousand voices tweet unseen, the dark rejoicing with their cheer -
the chant of crickets numberless, that stirs the thickets murmurous,
with ecstasies of melodies, of evening music amorous.

A chorus with harmony as smooth as sweetest symphony in tune;
as mild and tender in the dim as pale and slender light of moon;
with life infusing dead of night that drapes the musing silence round;
the heart beat of the slumbering plains, a gently lapping sea of sound.

A peaceful world of thought this brings, a world now furled in
lulling tide;
and while the tired body rests, the mind is fired and roving wide;
away from aching pangs that gnaw, and clouds that waking day
connives,
in tranquil sounds of reverie, until the glare of dawn arrives.

THE VALLEY OF MELANCHOLIA

The sky is charged; a veil of frozen dew
enshrouds the earth; the distant hilltops wear
the evening's pall of sullen, sable hue.
Still is the wind. With cries that fill the air,
the haunted voices of the valley share
their secrets awful and enthralling,
of nameless sins and tales appalling,
at which the trees would shudder, the mountains tremble -
with madness laughing is the moon,
conspiring stars bestrew the noon;
something of eeriness pervades
the raw and rugged rocks, the groves and glades.

Who wonders through this valley desolate?
Who, straying late, did Sorrow once accost,
and lead them here? Who came to contemplate
life's mysteries, whose searching hearts had crossed
into this land of doubt – but the path lost?
Up to the heavens they gaze – the vast
and lightless void, that us has cast
on inhospitable seas – they gaze with restless wonder -
but to their burning questions why -
it only echoes in reply;
for them no dogma bears a gleam
of truth that eases life's unquiet dream.

What spirits tread here, delicate and keen?
Spirits that beauty sought with eager eye -
who, finding it furled around a passing scene -

felt ecstasy - twined with a wistful sigh -
as naught the ebbing tides of time defy.
What piper there – whose plaintive sound
the valley echoes far around,
pipes of passing life and love and innocence?
What rhymer in the meadow sings,
sings of the passing of all things,
notes sad as solitary winter bird,
that through the velvet twilight drift unheard?

I knew a soul, on simple pleasures grown,
who of the springs of nature asked not how,
nor why, but trusted all he saw; unknown
lay tangled woods of knowledge near - his brow
unclouded still in youth's long dawn. But now
that unrefined and artless faith
has vanished like a fleeting wraith;
exiled from innocence, now sibling of the shadows,
his soul seemed like a hollow shell
where oceans deep of anguish swell;
in suffering's solitude he read
departed minds, and moved among the dead.

A yawning, overflowing emptiness
sighed through the valley's narrow, winding ways;
phantasmal howlings pierced the wilderness,
and beating wings of birds unseen would daze
his weary senses, shattering the haze.
Sometimes despondency became
half-pleasing – soft as candle flame;
at other times it cold and comfortless would grow,
and gleamed as hard and real as bars,
while hope lay distant as the stars,

and then stampeding herds of thunder
with sudden roll would cleave his mind asunder.

When nightfall in the valley would arrive,
he rested deep within its forests dim;
sleepless he saw its shadows come alive -
the puppets of the night stood tall and grim,
whose mocking voices would encircle him -
yet though this blackness round him crept,
still hope a tireless vigil kept.
One day he climbed the valley's tenebrous crags and steeps,
and saw a rainbow subtly spun,
caught momentarily by the Sun,
within a mist clothed waterfall,
dispersing colours myriad on all.

Since straying in valley long ago,
two voices call him - voices worlds apart;
one from the rainbow - hope's eternal glow,
the other - deep despair's untruthful dart;
both equal reign within his tender heart,
as how the mind contains such scope
for misery - yet equal hope;
as though the voices of the valley call no more -
and though, when downcast, he can find
that rainbow gleaming in his mind -
still, he can sometimes dimly hear
the frantic beating wings of madness growing near.

A NIGHT ON THE MOORS

The final embers flicker in the grate -
the murmuring ghosts of ravenous flames,
that licked the logs to ashes, that have warmed
this sharp November night – the only sound
rippling this stillness, save the ticking clock,
and faint stirrings of the dog. I listen -
a forgotten sound I can hear - the sound
of silence. And the city noise and heat
that weaves its fabric round my days - a hum
of blurred comings and goings, of bustle,
restless voices, footsteps, traffic – this I
noticed not - till now - when I hear it not.

How unquiet was my mind - how little -
swept in the city's unceasing torrent -
did I stop, and notice life? But alone
in this calm retreat, all around I hear
nature's subtle melodies – the river's
soft trickling in the darkness, the crunch
of leave-clothed paths on an afternoon walk,
the gentle winds which these walls encircle;
or see nature's art in colours blended -
yellows, greens and browns – mixed in harmony;
or cottage, brook and bridge a painting form.
In this seclusion I seem to find
a rustic philosophy, that teaches
something of silence and attentiveness;
a philosophy that these hills express
with more eloquence than the choicest words.

Soon I must leave, leave for the bustle,
yet still I'll hope within my heart to hear
the trickling river, the tick of the clock,
and the embers murmuring in the grate.

SNOWBOUND

One morning a visitor had arrived;
that night a blizzard had orchestrated
the whirling snow into a symphony,
and by break of day, the familiar roads,
paths, hedges, gardens of our town now slept,
buried beneath a mantle of pure white.

Startled was nature to a dumb silence,
expelled were the winds to their caves.
Waist high curved the snow, half way up the door,
falling through as we opened it; the dog
leapt with a wild excitement - normal life
was suspended, as roads and schools were closed.
Our world felt a bubble, its troubles
banished, as we played on sledges, finding,
in the cobbled streets of our routine days,
a new world to see, with eyes fresh as the snow.

But deep snow doesn't fall here anymore,
when children play in the streets, when sledges
slide down the hills; each year I hoped for it,
but hoped in vain, until I hoped no more.

BY A WATERFALL

Only the lone, resounding roar,
of waters that you tireless pour,
breaks this solitude, silent and still,
as you your ancient task fulfil -
of fresh ablutions at your shrine,
with waters pure and crystalline,
that clamorous the canyon flood,
while bearing homeward nature's blood.

A traveller, in winter's reign,
once stood upon this treeless plain;
thrilled by remote, secluded lands,
unseen, untouched by human hands;
with wild excitement he caught sight
of nature in her noble might,
seen only by a straying bird,
or passing tribesmen with their herd.
The traveller is seen no more,
while still the valleys hear that roar.

Since faded, unrecorded ages,
of shepherds, emperors and sages,
whole nations rise, decay and fall,
but steadfast stands this waterfall;
still bridging valley, hill and shore,
still with your lone, resounding roar.

TWO CITIES

Tonight I saw two cities side by side,
walked nameless backstreets by the day forgot;
saw blank and faceless windows hollow eyed,

behind closed shops that snarled together squat;
heard silent screams that pierced white heated nights,
that stirred the trash the strewed the empty lot.

The city's breath half veiled her neon lights,
veiled buildings tenanted only by the crow,
who pensive seemed from strange unearthly sights.

Those watchful streets my inmost secrets know,
as whispering, my every move they mark.
Then crunching through the crisp and gleaming snow,

warm windows bright I passed that cheered the dark,
as on my way I wondered, homeward bound,
relieved to hear the early morning lark.

The trees seemed tense - unable to expound;
tonight while walking I two cities found.

DO NOT WAKE HIM

Some say there is a changeless realm beyond -
more real - where life's Ideals like glaciers gleam,
and all things earthly with them correspond
as lesser shadows of this fettered dream.

But if they're right I do not wish to wake -
I hold a stolen piece of it in you;
and though for you my pipe can only make
poor echoes of its songs – I hope they'll do.

THE IDLE HOURS

The Idle Hours have found me out once more,
preyed on my straying thoughts - to murk and mire
you've cast them down in chains; lured by your lyre
they pace across the starless moors and shore.

You candle – like the flame of time you glow -
absorbed, unflinching as the gleaner stern -
time's wax its cull; say, have I wax to burn
for Idle Hours - say are you friend of foe?

Once more these unembodied voices stir –
sighs from the depths, the legacy of years;
would I could - when their chorus drowns my ears -
could drink forgetfulness - sink in its blur.

Below waves break on these rocks exposed -
cold snarl of rocks - what hands could fashion you -
what deity such monstrous chaos hew -
while skies in majesty remain reposed?

The candle draws me back; away from me -
you Idle Hours - soft-summoned by this leisure,
weaving your web of half-indulgent pleasure -
away from me – you perilous luxury.

TWO FLOWERS

Two kinds of flowers are in life's garden sown -
the first are words and deeds that spread a name;
for laurel wreaths and eulogies they're grown
that blow such blossoms of the mind to fame.

The second are the flowers of the flesh -
their tenders wish beyond the grave to be
borne down their children's children's bloodlines fresh;
both seek one trophy - immortality.

But fame like footprints washed by time shall fade,
and ancient houses one day heirless lie;
mock coins for dreams sublunary are paid
as growers vainly grasp a vacant sky;

yet what a greyness it would be to view
the garden coloured not by flowers like you.

OVER OCEANS ROARING

Higher and higher over oceans roaring -
vain was your writhing – captured, fevered snake;
this bird you yearned for - whose claws were knawing
deep in your heart – claws that your thirst might slake -
has dropped you on the waves that heedless break.

ON THE UK LEAVING THE EU

Though ages leave your chalk white cliffs unchanged -
were I a traveller, they'd not prepare
my spirits for the scene that waits – estranged
your broken days I walk, days full of care;
no dawn dispels the curling fog you wear,
drifting the oceans rudderless – a ship
no captain helms, while through the twilight air
comes luring, voiceless songs - lulled in their grip
the crew in two unruly bands has split,
while jagged rocks you skirt between unmanned -
a passage perilous, round isles that sit
in mists phantasmal, tempting hope for land -
the hope - on bleak horizons, growing near -
a paradise uncharted might appear.

THE PILLAR OF TEARS

It was an Eastern cistern underground -
a chamber filled with columns; once the key
to waters pure - slaves built it for the free;
a patterned pillar yet unchanged was found
whose frozen tears seemed but to break in sound -
the tears were notes – a silent symphony
of suffering they made - a melody -
that haunts the dimness with each spirit's wound.
Their voices formed a chorus - this they sang:
'We are the ghosts of tired limb and mind;
how tedious did our despot ruler find
our sorrows - he whose name down ages rang;
the hidden world in life we drifted through,
while monuments majestic shrine the few.'

ON ANIMALS

Earth, water, air and fire – creation's daughters -
that ceaseless merge and melt into each other -
as all is one – and he who creatures slaughters
is well to think he kills a distant brother,

for all the winding threads of life are bound
into the web of destiny; if changes
aren't just in earthly flesh and matter found,
but souls departed likewise make exchanges -

perhaps one day on us is raised the hand
with blade or hammer, if one were a bull
or swine or sow, that ranging on the land
knew not its grisly fate before the cull.

DRINK NOT TOO DEEP

If beauty be a tingling taste of terror -
drink not too deep; for he who tempted delves
in the beyond - may see a land in error
where unimagined horrors find themselves.
A statue once I saw – serene its face,
though round it one traced pain - the eyes
were fixed and riveted – a dreadful place
they spoke of - where the weight of ages lies.
His soul was a mosaic incomplete -
its fragments long he sought in far-flung realms;
there new pleasures would his senses greet -
forbidden fruit and spice that overwhelms.
An angel in a vision he was shown -
its beauty absolute turned him to stone.

SPIRITED UPON YOUR WINGS

Spirited upon your wings,
reveries bring boundless things;
with a pinch the sprightly fairy
blithely lures me while unwary,
guiding me with tuneful flute
round your orchards hung with fruit.

Vintages from caverns cool
brim in crystal goblets full -
sooth the spirit's civil strife,
nature's binding blood of life:
sun-soaked clusters bring the south -
rich with pulp indulge the mouth;
crushed in pressings lush and pure,
cast their rosy-woven blur;
comes the scent of nearby seas -
cornfields yielding to the breeze,
pipes I hear upon the mountains -
soon unlock the Muses' fountains,
then the hush, the moon, and me
make a goodly company,
joined by hoots and trickling brooks
mixed with music, thought and books.
Spicy malts bring woods and farms,
scenes unfold with rustic charms -
minstrels singing homely lays,
shepherds whistling on their ways;
next a tournament with lances,
then to evening country dances -

later gather round the fire,
hush-toned ghost tales 'til we tire -
creatures strange that cause affright
playing tricks to pass the night,
in enchanted forests lost
gleaming with a midnight frost;
sprites and goblins stray unseen
round the fresh-trimmed bowling green,
after village curfew knells -
local myths the parson quells;
Ursula - soothsayer old -
reads what yet the stars may hold,
from her mossy cave sees most,
tracing heaven's wakeful host.

Spirited upon your wings,
reveries bring boundless things;
guiding me with tuneful flute
round your orchards hung with fruit.

EVER BRUSH AWAY THE SLEEP

Ever brush away the sleep
that around the mind may creep -
not the one of lunar hours
when it flies to airy bowers,
but the slumbers oft that steal
over waking eyes they seal -
stealthy elf that leads it stray,
blind to high delights of day.

As the treasures of the mind
need we seek not far to find -
for in forest, field or hill,
native charms might senses fill
with undying, deep delight -
banishing the psyche's night;
wonders chanced in earth or skies
startle open eager eyes,
while the keenest ears discover
flowers laughing with each other;
scents of lilies, daisies, roses,
stir and quicken wakeful noses -
riches of the beggar's world,
that in visions near lie furled.
Sometimes though such pleasures seem
fleeting rainbows of a dream,
towers carved on clouds from ice,
which our hopes like moths entice,
when beguiled by phantom flames
soon a nameless grave them claims.

Long those towers lie submerged
seized by waves that seethed and surged -
spirit-wrecks in oceans sunk,
that of dark despair had drunk.
Greyer days of late left hope
like a fallen mirror broken -
shattered dreams in fragments lay,
wherein mock reflections play.
Yet the mirror tells but lies,
but deceives the psyche's eyes -
just a rousing sound or sight
animates the soul with light -
worlds of wonder soon are born -
hear these birds now herald dawn -
sleeper – wake - the kingdom's won -
see those fragments leap in one -
buried wrecks from depths will rise -
towers of ice on clouds will rise -
morning breaks – come see the dove
joyful circle skies above -
come climb mountains castle-crowned -
view the silvered scene around.

Ever brush away the sleep
that around the mind may creep -
stealthy elf that leads it stray,
blind to high delights of day.

THE CHILDREN OF THE SERPENT

Gales are gathering around your towers that lie crumbling -
bolted gates and doors seem poised, the stained-glass windows
restless rattle -
yet to revelry they're lost - deaf to the distant rumbling -
children of the serpent – born of warriors once formed for battle.

Leafless trees – whose boughs in frost are bound – you upwards
reach the skies
in frozen supplication – grey these days are where of late
only weeds bestrew the soundless wilderness; no birds arise
warbling at dawn to rouse the landscape dull and desolate.

Steadfast knights within still standing, silent in the gloom yet ready -
though now looming statues - yet your oath of duty knows not death;
would you stir from dreams unbroken, stir to meet this present eddy?
would to see your fallen children give your marble warmth and breath?

Ancient house secluded - these gold-fringed tapestries your deeds
narrate -
splendid halls were warmed by roaring fires of myth, while you
would dine
over tables boasting banquets rich; to lutes and lyres you ate -
then round Eastern carpets spun from silk raise chalices of wine.

You have tumbled to decay - a family line degenerate;
blind with idle words of fork-tongued flattery they cannot see -
lured by ease and sweet temptation's taste they shun the temperate
and sensation seek – with eyes that reel in frenzied ecstasy.

Shaken house - frail-shouldering these unchained elements - below
villagers would hear unholy shrieks come piercing through the night;
fearful of their feudal lords they pale and terrified would grow,
with unutterable secrets that would give the dead affright.

Where are your children, silent knights? To fields and hills they're gone,
there in orgies of sensation revelling; down pathless days
they have strayed. A kingdom rich with fruits forbidden they have won -
late beneath the moon with songs and dance carousing in a craze.

But the distant murmurs of unresting heavens passed unheard,
while in pleasures lost they heeded not. Nor heed they now the cry
of advancing blasts and hail – the trumpet calls of nature spurred -
whose pealings tell the tempest is at hand – and cannot lie.

In these walls retreated they; with fantastic mascarades
they divert themselves; among the statues of their mighty dead -
ancestors honoured long and far – they solace find; by colonnades -
filled with monuments of glory days – their fantasies are fed -

but now midnight strikes – above a crack of rolling thunder rings -
motionless - at games and quaint amusements they no more contrive;
every bolted door and stained-glass window sudden open flings,
as they shudder with an inward chill to see the storm arrive -

then a violent tremor shakes the earth – the walls and towers quake -
cracks appear and widen round the halls – foundations undulate -
tapestries disintegrate in flames while lavish mirrors break -
as the building trembles with a certainty that tells its fate.

Yet they cannot flee - forever more - for they have turned to stone -
statues now they are - frozen their faces as the ceilings fall;
lightning strikes - the building falters with a deep and primal groan -
then collapsing on the children of the serpent buries all.

IN DESPONDENCY

The gifts of life that fall for some in place -
the waterdrops and rays that some perceive,
which beams of friendship, love and purpose trace,
gifts that might rainbows of contentment weave -

they never did for me. Their paths I crossed
seldom – their colours glimpsing; to elope
with them I wished – from hours listless and lost -
but soon they vanished – taking with them hope.

EMELIE

Your gates are open – Emelie,
your turrets are unmanned;
across the gleaming moat I see
you wave with welcome hand.

No horses, arrows, swords or shields
for victory I need;
while bloodless stays the streets and fields -
your eyes I try to read.

But just the sound of your soft voice -
and I'm in shackles bound;
a happy slave that knows no choice,
who chains of gold has found.

You're waving still – I halt to choose -
as near to you I draw;
to force retreat – or win yet lose -
but choose I can no more.

A BUTTERFLY I THOUGHT I SAW

A butterfly I thought I saw -
with snow-like wings the field explore;
the smiling grass you flitted on -
your fragile beauty caught my eye -
I then gave chase – with longing sigh -
but blinked then looked – and you were gone.

A spider in its place I found -
poised motionless; beneath – around -
was spread your soft, alluring web,
which with a thousand charms was wrought,
where helpless like a fly I'm caught -
snared in the lair of passion's ebb.

The spider fled – around my head
a boisterous bee I heard instead;
with clumsy curiosity
you caused commotion then me teased -
threatened to sting me if you pleased -
with piercing kisses shower me.

The bee vanished - last on my hand
I felt a beetle soundless land;
in nature's duties deep absorbed -
so delicate I feared to crush
your tiny dome of colours lush -
of quaintest red with speckles daubed.

All these things – Emelie – are you
and more - a puzzle with no clue,
a horde of creatures in a box;
yet each is neither right nor wrong,
just notes that form your varied song,
song rich with human paradox.

ON VISITING NORTH DEVON IN OCTOBER

There is an echo in these breaking waves -
these wailing gulls, these midnight winds that moan,
the unbroken silence of these caves -
the soundless echo of a soul alone.

There are reflections in these crooked faces,
these empty streets, these pregnant clouds that roll
through cheerless skies - and each reflection traces
the inner landscape of a downcast soul.

There is a kinship in these things that form
the chosen haunts and songs of Pensiveness;
so clouds - do not depart, Sun - be not warm -
take not this company of dreariness.

MODERN BARDS

Modern bards - when you strike the lyre
let me not trudge through sludge and mire,
lost in the forests dark and tangled
of your perspectives jarred and mangled,
encircled by a mist of verses
that no revisiting disperses.
Be like the oceans deep yet blue,
that diving often brings sights new -
where Psyche's creatures quaint and strange
with Muses' help their songs arrange:
bring feelings sensitive as seahorse,
as dignified and seldom coarse;
bring meditations of the turtle,
and wit that sharks like lightning hurtle,
or ruminations of the crab
in waters grey but never drab.
Be pure as piper in the valleys
(though you may write of streets and alleys),
who captivates each flower and tree
with raw, untaught simplicity.
Next be the alchemist who turns
base passions into gold - who yearns
to weave his dreams with earthy words,
where hopes ascend unbound as birds,
where thought-jeweled casements lie in wait -
else, if with words you wish to paint
the spirit's weariness or howl -
be musical as mournful owl.
Modern bards - bring not murky waters -

but fountains fresh from the nine daughters,
whose rain of light still sometimes showers
wider thoughts on twilight hours.

BIRD OF DESTINY

Cold is the air - still are the trees -
the clouds are streaked with red;
hushed are the birds as dusk descends
and here you find your bed.

A whirling bird above is shrieking -
the bird of destiny;
of midnight born, with plume as black -
unearthly thing to see.

A pawn you were in unseen quarrels
of vying deities;
this bird tells of what has been spoken -
the voice of their decrees.

Your shield is shattered - in your side
a spear has slaked its thirst;
though life is slipping rest is here
now fate has done its worst.

These rivers were your cradle sought -
this chosen land your bride;
a rightful heir had come but you
were blinded by your pride.

Like bulls whose horns are locked in battle
you fought with armour crashing;
the plains resounded with the echo
of armies blindly clashing.

These fields were red, were filled with cries -
the rivers ran with blood;
this bird descended, soon you fell,
with dull and sickening thud.

O bird of destiny – oft seen
when skies are rumbling;
on tombstones perched in weather foul
and rooftops crumbling.

It knows no song of harmony
to charm the glades and dells;
its shrieking is the melody
that destiny foretells.

The final sleep is creeping near,
the scene is growing dim;
its noise a dull and distant blur -
your only passing hymn.

You see a dank enfolding fog -
hear chains that dimly clink;
a murky river to be crossed,
forgetfulness to drink.

Cold are your hands, still are your eyes,
vanished is your voice;
your bride is lost - the fitful gods
have made their final choice.

BLEMISHES

My flower - do these blemishes you taint?
Do they betray the canker's cold caress
and call the sunset on your loveliness?
Does Mortality its crimson paint?
Whose bite corrupts your petals - chaste and quaint -
what serpent's loathsome lips might you aggress?
Have you been licked by creeping frostiness -
fatal embrace in which so soon you faint?
I've wondered much - but no - some spots reveal
the claws of sickness - but yours - yours complete
your charms unique; to cure would be to kill -
so stay the hand - such blemishes don't treat -
but greet as friends and leave them flourish long -
these shadows in your summer pride belong.

APPLE BLOSSOM GIRL

She's in the field, not in the valley,
and weaves a braid with fresh-blown flowers;
she's in the woods - not forests shady -
with nature's music passing hours.
She's by the lake, not by the ocean,
whose waters seldom know commotion;
she's in the garden, not the moors,
nor near the fall's majestic roars.

She has not passed from storm to peace -
no thunder ever shook her summer;
when passing I will never cease
to pause and hear this artless hummer.
Serene her temples as a sage,
though she's a dew-clad May in age;
she's dutiful as honey bee,
and labours lost in reverie.

Around her mouth a laughter dances -
I know not why – nor hunger to;
my soul's transparent in her glances -
she's ageless as these rocks in view.
She's fragile-strong as swooning swan,
as secret as the dappled dawn -
when in her cottage she has gone
her fountain ever trickles on.

ON SEEING AN OPEN CASKET

Disturb her not – she is not far;
she hears our voices – whisper low.
Death does not her beauty mar -
does not her candle wholly blow.

Her features almost break in movement -
her cheeks still hold their hues of pink;
her lids might open any moment -
her spirit hovers round the brink.

She's gone not to some far-off land -
this room itself rests her from strife;
disturb her not then - as we stand
not by a sight of death, but life.

ON SEEING MANCHESTER AT DAWN

The sky's as charmless as a filthy rag -
as daylight breaks, the traffic shuffles filed;
pavements are tired and littered, bins are piled,
the clay-like Sun's first smiles with sadness sag.
The city's ragged as a vagrant hag,
and seems a lightless land for souls exiled -
yet somehow by this sight I am beguiled,
my spirits roused that in dejection drag.
I did not see - so hushful in the stone -
this loveliness I unexpected meet -
see these subtle charms all of their own,
that play around each weather-beaten street -
see in these buildings - that like flesh and bone
stir and wake - the city's hidden beat.

THE GARDEN TOAD

One morning in my garden - as the mist
dissolved – a thousand apples ripe and gold
I eager saw, that hung from boughs of gold.
I pondered which to eat, when through the mist -

there squatting in the stiff and frozen grass -
I saw a thing – still as the dead – a toad.
I stood as still for long, until that toad
fled suddenly, and hid within the grass.

Though then those golden apples I did eat -
still it is lurking sometimes by those trees,
staying my hand, when I go near those trees -
when pondering which apples I will eat.

DOWN ON THE HEATH

Down on the heath I met my lover, by arches strewn with vines
and flowers;
we kissed each other, then took cover, from skies portending April
showers.
Well I remember then I said – as evening fell so still and solemn -,
that flames will out, if too much fed' - as shadows grew around
each column.

Down on the beach I met my lover, beneath the slate-skies of
November;
I took her arm - I did discover - within my heart a final ember.
But now it only could be said – as evening fell so still and solemn -
''the flame is out, since too much fed' - as winter grew around
that autumn.

TO LIBERTY

With scanty roots upon an earthen stove
you sup by homely hearth; for long you dwell
within this city, sip its public well -
they call you Liberty; for you they strove -
these citizens – and sought you to betrove.
Hushed now these streets have grown. Hear you that knell -
see you these swollen limbs that plague foretell,
like wildfire reaching cloister, square and grove.
A grim new suitor seeks these souls to wed,
to lure to feasts in villas built on fable -
its name is Tyranny; how soon it fed
on hearts that feel of late by you misled -
but flee not with them, keep your simple table -
else join the growing city of the dead.

THOUGHTS ON HOME WHILE ABROAD

England – I never thought I'd feel
this need for damp and milder days;
abroad I roam yet wish to steal
      from tiring rays.

Empty these southern climes now seem;
empty the sun, the sea, the leisure,
these passing souls. This former dream
      brings no more pleasure.

These shedding leaves announce September -
the birds depart - I wish to part.
These fading charms make me remember
      where springs the heart.

Give me your days of grey again -
the mists, the heavens overcast;
the crunch of leaves that clothe the lane -
      the wind's fresh blast.

Bring sharp and frosty nights indoors -
the warming meal, the mellow fire;
old routines of domestic chores
      I now desire.

Bring faces long familiar,
whose voices still a rooting give;
with these I find - now felt from far -
      I wish to live.

OLD TALES I HAVE TURNED

Old tales of knights and honour I have turned:
sat at baronial tables, seen a hall -
through plots I've overheard – now rise, now fall -
spied cloistered sighs, felt pangs of lovers spurned;
breathed thin-high epic airs - watched cities burned,
while noble foes charged to the trumpet's call -
yet there's a volume I most prize of all,
within whose breathing leaves much more I've learned.
Though when it speaks I wonder what is meant -
a guileless language in its eyes I see -
wherein I trace the passions' firmament;
she is my class - her face is nature's key
to learning other volumes but augment -
she is this book - the heart's academy.

COULD I CAST SPELLS

Could I cast spells – antique and gilded cup -
clay guardian - whose tableaux chronicle
these fishermen their sea-nets lifting up,
these foxes eyeing gleans in baskets full -
clay man-at-arms - that battles time's keen edge,
that shields from its advance this pastoral scene
of two pale youths in rivalry to pledge
their hearts to her that tends the orchard green -
could I cast spells – in tableaux I would freeze
those moments spent with you that time lays waste -
those eyes that danced like light on summer seas -
where refuge from mortality they'd taste;
eyes that only memories have kept,
until towards oblivion they're swept.

ON SEEING THE AOSTA VALLEY

To add more notes to birdsongs would – I know -
only mar the passing hearer's bliss,
more hues just cloy the glory of the rainbow;
monarchs crowned would little gain or miss
if crowned once more for show – while here below
this scene is such that art I can dismiss.
Tranquil it sits in winter's parting chill:
the shops and cafes of the village seem
drowsy with sleep; surrounding mountains gleam
with fading snow; only the churchbells fill
the alleys hushed and calm; all life is still,
ruled by the rhythm of the gentle stream -
low clouds enfold the valley in a dream,
as we stand and watch it from the hill.

TWO SPRINGS

Two springs we drink from, since the days we met:
one is a silver stream – a draught brings joy,
transports me far to fields that never cloy,
where drowsed on flowers, I would time forget;
nearby – the next brings sorrow and regret:
turns fire to ice – turns to a scornful toy
a former love, whose charms now just annoy -
turns days awry, by sudden storms upset.
One lake of passion is for both their mother -
and with what bitterness we two have fought,
for our affections just to come to nought -
as when I drank from one, you drank the other;
and what a pity it would be - to never
drink from the silver spring of bliss together.

ON WAKING IN A VALLEY IN AVEYRON

Is it the nearby tread of furtive feet -
insistent in the darkness – or the sound
of nocturnal noses - probing the ground -
or trees - that rustle in this sleepless heat -
deep in this sudden solitude complete?
Is it a kinship that perhaps I've found
with nature when it stretches far around -
discovered in this stumbled-on retreat?
I do not know; and yet I can't remember
feeling such wonder in this thrilling measure -
my heart's rekindled like a dormant ember,
restless with a child's impulsive pleasure -
like on a festive morning in December -
and here are gifts indeed – in nature's treasure.

THE VILLAGE PLAGUE

With wordless murmurs, clasped in agonies of pleasure,
they huddled in amorphous masses by the river;
writhing they gorged on joy and pain in equal measure,
waiting for the one thing that would them deliver.

Grotesque and bulging boils and sores their bodies ravaged,
while vacant eyes and grins told of their minds devoured;
impassive slimy creatures soon among them scavenged -
the dumb and dogged worm virginities deflowered.

How swiftly had you come from Oriental lands -
Angel of Death – amid them moving stealthily;
unheard your trackless tread, unfelt your hoary hands,
yet in your wake they scattered to this colony.

As ravenous as wolves that spy the lamb they drank -
drank pleasures of the flesh, and feasted on themselves;
so near to death they little cared how low they sank -
but took their fill of life – for there was nothing else.

There were not graveyards wide enough to house them all -
their village was their cemetery; forsaken there -
no passing bells would sound, no hands would lay a pall -
no mourners now were left to spare a tear or prayer.

TO FRIENDSHIP

The bee-loved foxgloves could not charm the mead -
geraniums their full-lipped petals fend
against first frosts - bright roses not ascend
the cottage arbours – if they did not feed;
the peonies' brief buddings won't succeed,
nor irises, round the borders, with them blend -
yet there are plants I have not need to tend,
and you – my friend – are such a one indeed.
Be that the soil is damp or parched from drought -
like spring you're always fresh – my sure bed-fellow -
if no sun's near, your stems won't seek it out;
your leaves shall never wilt, grow sere or yellow,
but ever crown the garden - standing stout
through all four seasons – leaves no autumns mellow.

THE HORSEMEN OF THE NORTH

Riding the clouds of the turbulent skies -
clamourous hooves are your gathering voice,
mingling fast with your ominous cries -
thunder and lightning's your music of choice;
even in battle your honour not dies -
but in the land of the dead will rejoice.

Melded your flesh with the armour's cold metal,
skeletal features are twisted like sinew;
muffled the winds that the trees now unsettle -
horses are snorting - as blinkered they view
landscapes askew - while the hues of the petal
tear them apart in disorder anew.

Dreadful the din that has shattered each nerve -
muddied and bloodied the fields lie in stench;
blindly with fervour your leaders you serve,
guarding with duty the castle and trench;
yet in this carnage your loyalties swerve,
even while arrows their appetites quench.

Where are they now - that have fractured the state -
rotting its core – polluting each thought -
poisoning hearts with this burgeoning hate?
Distant the voices this massacre brought;
yet for the pageants and pomp of the great
father with son - son with father has fought.

Triumphant horsemen - how little you cheer;
dank are the fields that are graves for the young -
mangled they lie by the sword and the spear.
Though by your children these deeds will be sung -
filled are their dreams with your legacy fear -
dreams where such horrors once dormant are sprung.

www.ingramcontent.com/pod-product-compliance
Lightning Source LLC
Chambersburg PA
CBHW031422160726
47993CB00003B/1350